Life of Spike

James R. Bower

Copyright © 2019 James R. Bower

All rights reserved. No part of this book may be reproduced or transmitted in any form or by any means, electronic or mechanical, including photocopying, recording or by any information storage and retrieval system, without permission in writing from the publisher.

Average Dog Publishing- Deer Park, TX
ISBN: 978-1-7337590-3-8
Title: Life of Spike
Author: James R. Bower
Available Formats: eBook | Paperback distribution

THIS BOOK IS DEDICATED
TO A VERY SPECIAL DOG
SPIKE

SEPT. 1973 - FEB. 1993

About the Author

James R. Bower, retired designer of architectural and mechanical engineering, a U.S. Paratrooper Veteran of the 60's and 70's. I now spend my time getting back to my artwork pencil drawing and painting. I used to raise horses, cattle and buffalo on my ranch in Texas but retired from that also. I was born and raised in Michigan, I moved to Texas in 1981. I'm married with 5 kids, 12 grand kids and 4 great grand kids.

Spikes Life Story

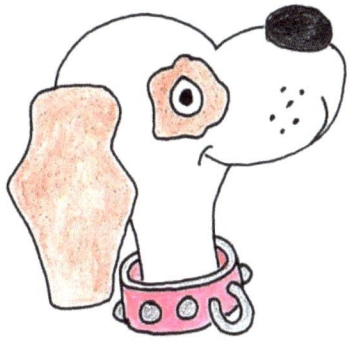

Spike was born outside a small town called Clifford in the state of Michigan. It was the year 1973, the month of September. I had two small children, the oldest a boy and the youngest a girl. I figured it was time they had a little dog to play with and learn the responsibility on how to care for one. I found an advertisement in the paper stating free puppies. We all jumped in the car to go see the puppies.

When we arrived, we found out there were only two puppies left, one was Black and White and the other one was Brown and White. We were going to have a hard time choosing which one we wanted.

We had the owners keep them on one side of the room and the kids on the other side. The kids called the puppies to see which one would come to them first. That's how Spike became ours, he was the one who came up to them first. Spike now has a new brother named Jeremy and a new sister named Laney. Spike sure loved the attention he received right away.

As time went by, we moved to another small town in Michigan called Silverwood. Spike loved it there because the house had 20 rooms and 3 1/2 acres of land for him to roam around and explore. One silly thing he would like to do was to sit on the corner of my drawing board while I was working.

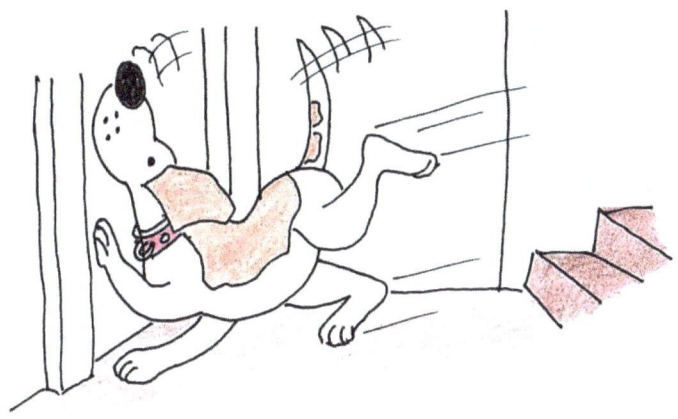

One evening I was doing some artwork upstairs and decided to go downstairs for a cup of coffee. Spike decided not to walk downstairs so he jumped from the top step. When he hit the floor below, he slid across the foyer, he ended up landing against the front door. Funny, but lucky he didn't get hurt.

The front yard was full of Black Walnut trees. Why did Spike like this? Squirrels lots of Squirrels. He would stand in the front window and watch them playing all day long.

The house was built back in 1861 as a stagecoach stop. the house came complete with a few bullet holes in the walls. To say the least, it was a little spooky at night. One evening, Spike and I stayed there by ourselves. He slept on the bed between me and the doorway. He slept with one ear perked up because we could hear a lot of noises. Of course, I believed it was the squirrels in the attic.

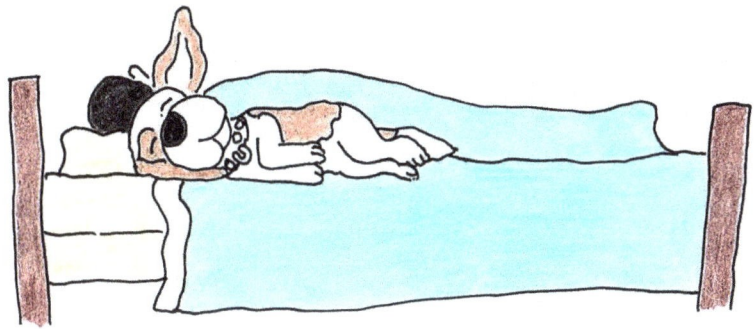

As years passed by, we moved to another small town in Michigan called Kingston. It was farther out into the country. Spike liked the country because it gave him more room to explore. Spike got to meet the neighbors Golden Labrador. They seemed to get along great.

Spike also like to chase little field mice. He got to where all I had to say was mouse and he would run all over, looking for a mouse. He liked looking through the wood pile for mice.

On a cold winter day Spike decided to take off with the neighbors Labrador and some other neighboring dogs. He was gone for three days. I drove around showing his photo trying to see if anyone had seen him. On the third day I came home from work. As I was getting out of the car, I saw my neighbor standing on her back porch waving at me. She opened the door, and out, Spike ran on a dead run across the field. I gave him a hot bath, a few cookies and a cup of coffee. He went to bed and slept for hours. He had gotten so cold his ears had frost bite.

Spring came along and his next exciting adventure came one evening when I let him outside. Just as I turned the porch light on, he went down to the bottom of the steps. Just as he got settled down, a big shadow completely covered him up. A big barn owl swooped down and tried to pick him up. If I wouldn't have been there, the owl would have gotten him.

Again, we packed up and moved to a town outside of Houston Texas called Pasadena. For starters, we had to move into an upstairs unit of an apartment complex. Spike and I both didn't like that because we are country boys. We sure didn't care for apartment buildings. But of course, you had to start somewhere. That's where Spike didn't like living on the top floor. He also didn't like the heat. I had a hard time getting him to go outside. Finally, he got use to all that and started making a lot of friends around the complex.

The time came to buy a new home, it had a nice big back yard for Spike and the kids to play outside in. That's where Spike first learned about fire ants. I had heard him barking at the back door. When I opened the door, he was standing there all covered in fire ants.

I grabbed up Spike and put him into the shower. I turned the water on full blast to rinse the ants off him. After all that he decided not to go around anymore ant hills.

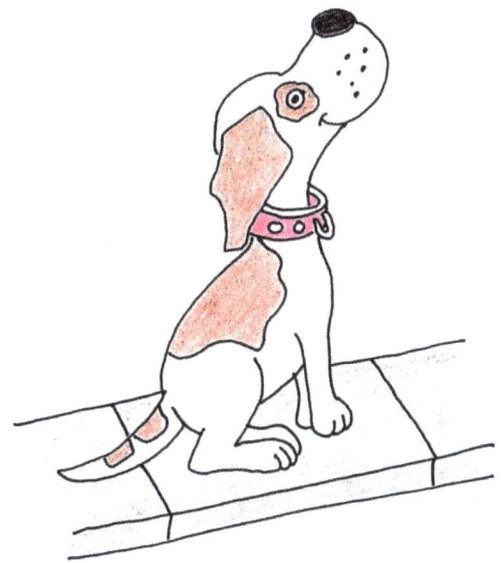

Spike made friends with the neighbors next door. When ever he came up missing, I knew they had called him over. They would feed him steak and anything else he liked.

With life changes, the kids, Spike and I moved back to the apartment complex. They were the same apartments that my two sisters lived in. Spike liked it because he made even more new friends. Spike also got to stay with his Uncle Gary, Aunt Nancy and his cousin Josh during the day while I was at work. Spike really enjoyed staying and playing with Josh. He spent a lot of his time under Josh's highchair cleaning up the food Josh would throw down to him.

A few years later I got re-married and we moved to a townhouse in the same complex. Spike now has a new mother Carlotta, two new sisters, D' Angela and Karla. He also got a new brother Craig. Spike loved all the new attention he got. He got to go to the park a lot more now. A few months later we got to buy a house just down the street from the park.

My wife brought her dog Keshie to the new house. Spike and Keshie got along just fine. Keshie ended up having surgery so Spike was kept away from her after she got home. Spike wasn't going to have that. We finally let him in the room with her. He would go up and nuzzle her, then went over to her bowl and got a mouth full of food. He walked over and laid the food down in front of her so she wouldn't have to get up and eat.

A few years went by and we lost Keshie. It was very hard on Spike because he was getting very old. The Veterinarian told us that we had to keep a close watch on Spike because he's so depressed. He was very attached to Keshie.

Then one day the girls were playing in the front yard and a little Siamese kitten came up to them. The girls of course, wanted to keep the kitten. We couldn't find where she came from and nobody was looking for the lost kitten. Spike got a new friend called YoYo.

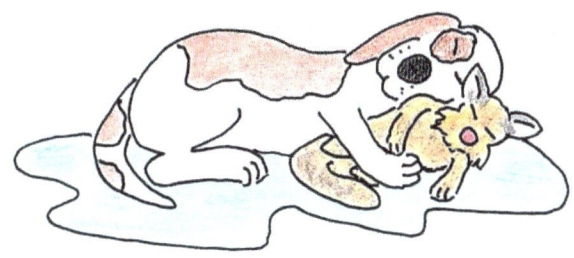

YoYo actually adopted Spike as her parent. She followed him around like a shadow. Spike and YoYo slept together, ate together and played together. Spike had a life that most people would have liked to have. He had a great 19 ½ years. YoYo was really lost without him. Everyone who knew and loved him sent me pictures that they had of him. I now have a big photo album of him. Spike will live on forever in our hearts, and in his series of books.

www.ingramcontent.com/pod-product-compliance
Lightning Source LLC
Chambersburg PA
CBHW040109100526
44584CB00029BA/4016